drift

ALSO BY KEVIN CONNOLLY

Asphalt Cigar
Happyland

drift
KEVIN CONNOLLY

poems

Lynner
I like this one, even
if you didn't edit it.
Thanks for all the support
xo
"Trillium Man"

ANANSI

Published in 2005 by
House of Anansi Press Inc.
110 Spadina Avenue, Suite 801
Toronto, ON, M5V 2K4
Tel. 416-363-4343
Fax 416-363-1017
www.anansi.ca

Distributed in Canada by
Publishers Group Canada
250A Carlton Street
Toronto, ON, M5A 2L1
Toll free tel. 1-800-747-8147

Distributed in the United States by
Publishers Group West
1700 Fourth Street
Berkeley, CA 94710
Toll free tel. 1-800-788-3123

09 08 07 06 05   1 2 3 4 5

LIBRARY AND ARCHIVES CANADA CATALOGUING IN PUBLICATION DATA

Connolly, Kevin
Drift / Kevin Connolly.

Poems.
ISBN 0-88784-727-7

I. Title.

PS8555.O554D74 2005   C811'.54   C2005-900645-5

Cover design: Bill Douglas at The Bang
Cover photograph: Eamon Mac Mahon
Typesetting: Brian Panhuyzen

Canada Council
for the Arts

Conseil des Arts
du Canada

ONTARIO ARTS COUNCIL
CONSEIL DES ARTS DE L'ONTARIO

We acknowledge for their financial support of our publishing program the
Canada Council for the Arts, the Ontario Arts Council, and the Government of
Canada through the Book Publishing Industry Development Program (BPIDP).

Printed and bound in Canada

(finally!) for Gil

Contents

drift

ABOUT A POEM

It's all so glamorous — the waiters, the bookkeepers,
the chandeliers, the rock stars reviewing the Best
Westerns of the Arctic Circle. Between tables,
the actors are working on their "motivation."
"Think of the steak as conflict, the three-peppercorn
sauce as a life lesson," a pretty blonde tells the maitre d'.
"It's all about *process*, process is everything."
I've been thinking about the librarian as sex symbol.
Is it the spectacles, I wonder, or their removal?
The trussed hair, or its liberation — unkempt,
straying over eyes struggling for focus?
A waiter passes and I order a gimlet,
not because I have a clue what a gimlet is,
but because it sounds so damned Shakespearean.
Such are my whims, such are my frivolities.

It all reminds me of John Ashbery's poem
"The Tennis Court Oath." Not the poem,
really, because who can remember poems,
except for parts of "The Hollow Men"
(and I don't think that should count).
It had something to do with Cromwell or
the French Revolution — "The Tennis Court Oath,"
that is — though I'm actually reading something
completely different at the moment, Anne Carson's
Autobiography of Red, which is so, like, Greek to me,
I wish it was *The Autobiography of Red Skelton*,
whose last name sounds a lot like "skeleton,"
reminding me I'd better drop in something witchy,
touching on mortality, perhaps, in the last

stanza here if I really want to pull this out
of its siren-screaming nosedive.
But I am no John Ashbery, no Bugs Bunny;
there'll be no cartoon gas tank conveniently
run down to empty two feet from fiery ruin.

Time for another gimlet, I'm thinking, though it's true
they're going down way too easy, what with all
that crème de menthe, or whatever it is puts the
gee whiz into that particular gin fizz. Sure,
I could look it up, just like I could have looked up
the Tennis Court Oath, but where's the fun in that?
As a pretty blonde between my ears reminds me,
it's all about process. So what say you grab yourself
a gimlet, push the peanuts over my way, thank you,
and we'll just kick back and enjoy the artistry . . .

ADDITION

It's all amusing, until you're
asked to laugh —

dancehalls, dunce caps, fence posts,
iron lungs, detritus

Snore it out between dreams, after horrors,
sweat wandering the neck —

bend it to a whim, a corridor, any
absence of composure

bone grown hard over emptying chest.
The lump on the springboard —

scent of anger, panic, then the inevitable
cannonball. A heart expands

despite itself: new rooms thundering over
the same stricken tenant

AND . . . SCENE

Citizens of earth, return to your homes!
Your lease has not yet fully expired. The stones
in the driveway are the same as yesterday's,
though not verifiably those of decades past.
Yes, change is inevitable, the sea lions riot but
their numbers wane, just the diehards now clutched
around the embassy shouting the old slogans — no
one serious pays them any mind. Go home, I tell you!

Shrimps seethe in the bay. Angry, sure, who wouldn't
be? Still, far from *murderous* as some of the papers shout —
not one tiny soul has called for blood. So, no worries.
Disperse and go about your normal business.
Nothing to see here but embers . . . that little
rope we use to haul the morning.

ARCHITECT

I imagine the corner as
four corners, on which
sit four traffic lights, four
blocks, soaring into four cubes,
four towers, overlooking
countless over-lit squares.

Thus is a life brought to ruin —
street by dreaming street.

AWARDS GALA

The mosquito receives the award for Best Insect That Sucks
(despite the backhanded slight he conducts himself with dignity)

A cockatiel cops Bird Whose Name Most Resembles a
    Mexican Entrée
(checks her tail for condiments and leaves the stage relieved)

A bent tenant grabs Best Impersonation of a Breathing Apparatus
(holds the trophy to his mouth and draws amused applause)

The flying buttress nabs Best Ornament in a Supporting Role
(the seventh straight year — she feigns surprise)

The award for Best Biological Redundancy goes to the hamate
bone (over the appendix, but we'll leave that debate for later)

During the ceremony it all seems fine, on the up and up —
the burghers win Best Burger, the ruffage gets Best Roughage —

until the rest of us roll home pissed, hoarse from shouting,
loser propping up loser, convinced the whole thing's rigged

CALMNESSES

I tell you now, I nurse no grudges.
It's great when we can mend things.
It's great that you've come around
to a way of thinking I think we can
all agree is neither herenorthere.

Calmnesses — another comely, clumsy
term for what we know ourselves to be
entirely lacklustre, but at least we agree on
the term for it: *Camelnesses*.

Think of a hump, in the middle of a desert,
with no riddles — not even Nelson Riddle,
whose name itself puts the lie back in likeness,
and as you're no doubt sick of hearing,
I've disliked ourselves for some time now.

THE CARDIGAN OF JEANNE D'ARC

That night up in the Crow's Nest Lounge, some odd ducks
claimed they'd never even heard of chocolate. Which was
especially disturbing to the Easter Bunny, who
had always considered the work a public trust, and was
soon seen sobbing into a pint of Old Speckled Hen.
Meanwhile, at a neighbouring table, Thomas Chester
Harrison, inventor of the windsock, tossed the last salty
tidbits from his can of chicken haddie into the fireplace.

"The cardigan of Jeanne d'Arc," he said, nodding
sombrely, while the flames turned our faces into frightful
cave paintings, and the Pigeon Homers League wrapped
him in that taut silence of which they're famously fond.
None of us would ever amount to anything — he
knew that, and we loved him all the more for it.

THE CARTOGRAPHER'S LAMENT

Their initial eagerness, then the disappointment on their
little faces when you tell them it's promontories not
dormitories, hills not thrills, ports not Port . . . or portfolios —
in short, that you have nothing they need screw you for.

Though you can't see why the essentialist should thrive:
draws a box instead of a square, blot instead of a circle,
spot on a globe, globe on a silly carousel, roaming speck on
a vorticist's dream of a cold, quiet, charismatic nada . . .

But no attention to detail — Yonge Street versus Old Yonge,
newcomers and Old Cummer, Grosvenor Square versus
Grosvenors Crescent and Place . . . Forget it, you'll chart
the ant farms anyway, greenhouse to townhouse to bungalow —

you've worked with illiterates before and got them all home in
one piece (-ish). Once the ones are counted, it's all about vocation
— who's on the hill, who's in the trenches — while the tenants
grouse and organize, haul fresh bodies home for dinner.

CHAIN:

Stare at the word long enough and you'll steal its
heart, blur its purpose, leave it stained and wintry
as empty buildings. Whereas an object is never
anything but itself — even if its light strays, variably,
its windows are thrown open, it is always occupied.

When things get away from you, they don't just
vanish, they stream off in chains, hand in hand,
small children hectored from playground to bus seat.
That night we met down by the lagoon beside the
miniature village, what species of night was that?

Was it ardorous or arduous? Funny, I can't remember,
just as I can't revive the names of storms or girls, though
they've both tongued me hotly, sent me reeling off to bed.
There are people who think and people who think ill,
those who reason and those who dream up reasons.

Then there are the others — insistent, empty, wet
with love — primed for a wink, a shape, a sneeze.
Be happy in this life, they say, tread its dormitories
briskly, deliver its speeches and wrongly addressed mail,
mate harmlessly, resist this terror of the random.

But if it's the *event* that's so important, why is it only the
untouched, the virgin — sealed toy, uncancelled stamp,
unused ticket — that holds value for the serious collector?
We reach for it, it moves. We collect ourselves. It moves
again. Six inches, one way or the other, and we starve.

CONTRACTUAL OBLIGATION

Good afternoon. I'm a little baby.
I know I don't look like a little baby,
but I can assure you that I am.
I thank you all for coming this evening.
I'd also like to thank this afternoon's sponsors:
the sun, walnuts, Parma ham, and
the woody permanence of chairs.
And I'm sure you'll join me
in expressing our sincere gratitude for
bending, stretching and branding,
for rain, wind and rectitude.

I'd like to thank you all for coming
on this windy evening, full of promise;
I'd thank you not merely
on behalf of myself, a little ham,
but on behalf of our guests — sun,
wind and the woody rectitude
of permanent rain. I'm grateful for
your gratitude, for your bending
and your wilting, and especially for
your support of our major sponsor,
Sunny Walnuts.

I'd like to thank you all for coming,
but remind you to clean up after yourselves.
Did I mention the little baby?
That I have the great good fortune of being
he on this rainy, woody afternoon?
Of course, quite right, I mentioned that
in closing, before we welcomed
our guests, but after we thanked our
sponsors: wind, rain and branding.

Thanks for coming, thanks. Really,
if you'd all just shut up and take your
seats, our breathless evening of thanks
and sincere gratitude might finally begin.
And now, ladies and gentlemen, I'd like to
turn your attention to the woody clearing
at the opposite edge of the stage.
On any other windy evening, it is rectitude that
would be sitting there, but of course,
on grounds I'm sure are repugnant to you
and I, both as loyal babies and as little hams
in our own right, rectitude is playing
rock hockey in a foreign country none of us
could pronounce correctly if we tried,
so let's stop trying, shall we?

Good morning. I'm a little baby.
I'd like to thank our sponsors,
who I believe you now know personally,
and I'd especially like to thank you all
for coming on this windy evening.
Thank you all. If you'd please, please,
please just take your seats in the
clearing, we're ready to begin.

DEATH BY SCANSION

Little girls gliding by on wheels can kill you.
Hospitals kill: weather, mosquitoes, dead birds . . .
Familiar sounds can kill you; wet barns, red and
subsumed by lilies. Thinking will kill you dead,
though it may never, and surely hasn't yet. Fast
food is lethal, as are brooding and regret, though
I've heard it's a slow, not entirely disagreeable death.
The latest Ashton Kutcher vehicle will kill you,

as will hope, job stagnation, a preponderance of
wind chimes, bad credit, bad drugs and drinking water.
Cows can kill when fed their own meat. Iris
DeMent kills 'cause she sings so damn sweet.
Rich kill poor, poor kill the riche, each
crime buried with its own little clique.

DEEP THOUGHTS AND IMPORTANT FEELINGS

If women gave birth through their noses there'd be
a lot more of those knife-happy pediatric surgeons a-
round, not to mention a healthy run on rhinoplastics —

such are the deep thoughts and important feelings
that rattle me lately, wake me at noon and
send me back to bed with the bag of Smartfood.

A snowflake racing toward the Great Divide,
as televised live on Headline News, has blessed me
with a newfound interest in extreme ironing, much

as the unprecedented popularity of George Foreman's
Lean, Mean, Fat-Loss, Thefuckitscalled Machine
has left me toothless, that is, without genuine tooth.

All of which suggests it's true, the Old World saying:
"When your beet's baked it's time to wash your tops,"
meaning, I suppose, "Call in all outstanding favours."

I never knew how hard it was to get fired until
I started working for the government full-time —
not to mention the perquisites . . . you know, the

perquisites: the tethered zeppelins, scream classes,
the buttered love-toys greased for each debriefing —
midgets, saddle sores, nude dancers, a waterfall . . .

DEPOSITION

Wreath of shadows
breathed-out in doctored
darkness, take my testimony.
Conjure truckjacks in a junkyard,
chill the runways in your
cave of white.

Cowl of door frames
lifeless in the noon sun,
drop your dark suit carefully.
Walk the gravel to the causeway,
whisper vengeance
to the shards of evening.

DOMESTIC LYRIC

Out west, it's so dry, the rain vanishes before it hits the ground.
That's heavy, dude, write a poem about it.

And that kitten, it glides over the hardwood like, I dunno, mittens.
That's heavy, babe, write a poem about it.

You know, Frida Kahlo, she did some fucked-up pictures of herself.
That's sweet, man, write a poem sequence *about it.*

And Hemingway blew his brains out when his dick wouldn't work.
Harsh! But are you thinking what I'm thinking? — Poem!

And Lewis Carroll, paddling around with all that underage tuna.
That's fucked-up, hombre, but a big *opening for a poem.*

Not to mention my ex-wife, sticking it to that grad student.
Miserable liar, what say we drop a poem on her?

And the November trees, they're like sad fingers, you know?
And that's such a freaking poem I totally can't believe it!

DOWN TO EARTH

Read backwards what's written seems hopeful.
A bell goes and begin again — wheels rolled
over wheels, a great commotion written forward.
Memos gather (task and problem), obstacles are thrown

up, examined, then brought down through some
colossal collective effort. In the afternoon it seems
calmer. You nap in the window where the day hangs
longer, watch dry grass gasp, embers of summer.

Everything's a gesture, a treatise on going forward.
There are broad arguments, checks and measures,
events fated and events clearly accidental.
There are clouds and the breaks between them,

through which pours light and what look like birds,
or leaves, or broken branches; souls, even (the poet
in you wants to say), singed and shaken, hurled
back to hard ground, a place that knows them.

DRIFT

There is so much Everything
that Nothing is hidden quite nicely.
　　　　　— Wisława Szymborska

The Killim Haus, Delia's Esthetics,
Shawarma Hut, all of them duck before
the same sullen pleasures —
the village of tomorrow undone
almost by accident, a loose coalition
of strip malls and strip malls and strip
malls: Quik-E Convenience,
Cheers Fine Foods, Fish and Cheeps —
a pet store. In the absence of real stars,
repetition has its consolations —
random lights conscripted into the opera,
reimagined as sheet-metal thunder,
Sea of Rains Dry-Kleen,
two-for-one Szechwan lobster.

What endures, a piece of it, is weather,
the snap and cuddle of clouds,
on-and-off pressure of traffic,
treasured debris of childhood
cohabiting the same shrunken rooms,
the same lint-frosted airducts,
same breezeway assignations after
bridge or curling or cribbage:
Where's Dad? Did Beth leave?
Who signed what in who's yearbook,
who conjured the calamity — the deep
tension-emptying sigh before
the garage door dumped its
gust of impossible light?

It's all good because it's all decided.
The dream mall closed for business,
its flummoxed architect returned
to Europe with his tale between his teeth.
But who'll hike out the salvage?
The anchor-stores crumbling, time-
shares stuttering, the buckling credit
of the jury truants: *No flyers, please;
No one home; Not at this address* —
all of it a tough-love lesson in
the pitfalls of earnest simulation.
Desperation among toothpicks,
unlit gatehouses, vacated parking
booths — hard edge trembling in
a wilderness of signs.

EELS

Through heavy darkness
the eels advance, cold
morning fathers who'd rather
run than fight. Their souls
are great tunnels, eyes
filled with dusk. Almost living
they are, groping after a
day's slow fingers.

It is futile to oppose them.
Pointless.

ERRATA

after Paul Muldoon

for silver read sliver
for valve read salve
for salve read slave
for slave read salvo

for champion read champignon
for flowers read Fowler's
for feign read reign
for error, terror

for calm read clam
for mussel, muscle
for drops read ropes
for ropes read tropes

for rain read drain
for a plum read aplomb
for a trifle read rifle
for balm read bomb

for slip read slap
for past read last
for lass read glass
for wine read wind

for insert read inert
for insect read insert
for dove read cove
for lover, hover

for scuff read scoff
for strife read strafe
for there read here
for scrabble, rabble

for chat read that
for for read four
for read read head
for head read hear

for hear read heart,
threat, thread, dearth,
and so on

FAMILIAL

Who needs it, all this hand-me-down?
Bent nose, frayed nerves, weak shore
of greying hair. What do I care if you spill
open recklessly, toss the attic again for
keepsakes you dreamt but are never there.
It's not easy, whatever people say —
to waste love knowing it comes rarely;
to dress nonsense in urgency;
walk the moon through its dopey paces;
to fall into the current dumbfucked and,
standing, find there's still room
for your head in this sorry world.

The dead remember, lest we forget them,
ticking in their caves of silence.

FINGER LAKE

There is a lake
in the scene above my body
no one dares to touch —
a question, a rumour
clothed in throaty silence.

From where I sit
drowning in the garden,
I can see my fingers
fish-hooked by its
briar of stars.

FORGERY

these bottomless days of which only drunks
speak glowingly rush blurring into the
fix of meaning — the thrum and dog-ear
the scratch and hijinks

or tacked like old doors to stained
petitions, bold slogans trending well
with semi-pros and old fuckers — the
sole respite, a forgery that cons us all:

a day that ends and ends and keeps
on ending, until one night it doesn't

GET WELL SOON

At least it comes sprightly, coins on
heavy grass, shaping and assessing
all it calls to order, slaps calm,
elbows into the mind's blind corners.

Pills, sentiments, the lung's window
opened on a body's wailing spaces.
Dwell here at your peril — kingfish
among the intoxicants. Watch it

fleshed out, for a moment at least;
time enough to lose your eyes, too,
slip inside with all those winds and
horrors we speak so well of most days —

well of ropes, well of ruckus, well of
reason . . . the well of Oh well.

THE GRADUALISTS

The live bootleg of *Heavy Metal Meltdown*
made them weep to a man, though they were
all shit-faced, and would probably have bawled
over a well-made button, or that particularly
persistent ad for microwave pizza. Still, it's a
cheap business blaming the victim: no challenge
for the intellect, no day job, at least not since
"someone" cooked up the letter bomb that
reduced head office to whistling rubble.

And none of this will change the fact
I need a new live-in cover girl, one who won't
sweep the cobwebs from the corners, who'll
sip the cheap cognac and listen to the stories
of the old days: the gnat that baffled Moscow,
the organ grinder's arrangement with the pontiff,
the gloves that ruled Boston like clenched fists.

Outside the window, the one that exists only
on this page, a misshapen cloud floats over
a cornfield, pondering a penknife.
Which is, of course, *wrong* . . .
what possible allure could whittling
hold for a meteorological triviality? Still, it's
definitely up to something, stealing away
like some stained cravat hog-wild for similes.

Ten years back I'd have set out after it,
but my petulance has faded over time,
and, alas, I have my own dalliances —
a reptile farm that requires constant policing,
the actuarial ticking of imagined check marks
on hypothetical forms as the cells expire
and collapse in the apiary of my bones.

And what then? After the predictable foreclosure?
Who will auction off the shimmering dreck —
the slow thoughts, the gradualists, with all
the stage presence of duelling pennies?
Who'll lower the frogmen into the aquarium?
Who will linger to tutor my days,
prepare them for their long march
into the terrible canyons of air?

HALF OF SOMETHING

. . . everything strains to be inevitable
even as it's being killed forever
                    — David Berman

Autumn drops and we need to leave
the futile thoughts alone, suffering out
their sanguine line of dropped stitches.

I knock my head against the gargoyle,
put a tongue in its ear, knowing what
that does to the withers and the wherewithal.

An urge to starch a window's brightness flat,
ivy and its intrigues, the doves' laundry
thrown to sea for good and ever.

No more talk of birds' bleach and freshman
spunk, we'll play out the dumbbell aria:
no wind, but the lake, it talks and talks . . .

I close the window on it, still it talks,
its half of something going on, shrugging
off objections, all those one-at-a-times.

Still, there's time left to save the effort,
or what spawned it, still time to become the
sort of man that type scorns, the kind that never

pauses, shuns complaint, never fails to pull its
two eyes out of its sockets, shadow the parking
lights into the blurring pupil of darkness.

HARD ABOUT

I have not strummed my eardrums wisely,
nor watered my nosegay of Tuesdays,
nor quietly stowed the sticky memories —
triumph in childhood (first to breathe), promise
in youth (the high-school bookie), success in
business, perversion in middle age, dickering
in dotage, and all set to another's compass: pigeon
tracks among the barkers and the sunflowers.

To be down with it however cheap the feathers.
To croon splendidly despite the gathering dirge.
To ring the optometrist's mantra: *Better like
this; better like this? Like this? Or this?*
To stop worrying what I really think.
What I really think is nothing.

HARMLESS RITUALS

Harmless rituals of summer:
aeronautical canopy of trees
jeered by passing clouds,
shiftless troupe of earwigs
preening for their encore —
a truncated eternity of
starlets and knitting needles.

Then, of course, there's Sven,
who speaks the language,
but has a weak grasp on
the principles of tanning:
the cramped unsanitary huts,
the toxic runoff into the watershed.

As luck would have it,
I'm carrying Grandma
in my fifth pocket,
sharing space with a
bus token and a forgotten
antihistamine —

"What about it?" I demand
over an uncomfortable
moment of silence. "You know,
the 'ironic counterpoise,'
the dance of all and nothing?"

"Watch the ducks," she bellows
through a promotional bullhorn for
the Festival of Breathing,
"the ducks see everything,"
and suddenly, almost by chance,
I think I've guessed exactly
what she might have meant.

HISTORY CHANNEL

The limo driver will be drugged *and* drunk,
the route preplanned, underpass carefully chosen,
paparazzi hired specifically for the crack-up —
no need to pull film from the cameras,
there was never any there in the first place.

The shots will come from the front. Bullets
will be planted, wounds doctored, autopsies
rendered incomprehensible. The chain of
custody will be sorely compromised —
golf bag gone missing, ice cream unmelted —

gloves and thumps and barking dogs.
The area will be air-access only, photos dodgy,
microchips too small to allow detection. The artists
leave fields under cover of darkness, key
witnesses meet with freak, untimely deaths.

Go ahead, dig up the rock star, he's long gone:
the homage graffiti, tombstone testimonials,
just wasted breath. The newspapers pitch
columns against us, ants pile the lies high
and deep; bees paper their cells with

whispers, gather poison behind their knees.
In the Scottish murk, the fins of ancient beasts.
In the Mojave, clear prints of a lunar lander.
A knife on the counter, voice on the wireless,
a nurse's shoes stacked neatly on the squad car.

HOOKS

after Darrell Gray

The hooks of panic and obliging bloodhounds.
The hooks of winter, torched ragged trees.
The hooks in the mirror, cramped, dumbstruck.
Amorous hooks, scuffling on escalators.

The hooks of kinship, the hooks of promise.
Solitary hooks hung in bent door frames.
Hooks that stir and shimmy down drainpipes.
The hooks of wonder and of doubt.

Meat hooks.
Paper hooks.
The hooks of obsolete species.
Hooks perched on a moment's peace.

Hooks of nightbirds, plotting against daybreak.
The hooks that groan in everything you touch.

IN LIMBO,

wild hares crawl up the ass of no one,
so breathe easy
in the cluttered vestibule.

There's time,
the day suggests, hopefully perhaps:
hot bright rusted grass.

Time revels in its gaunt celebrity —
all tilt and counterpoint,
a drowsy feather hovering in a maelstrom.

Like thunder dwarfing a stickpin,
or just a dogfly dodging water boulders
over a swollen culvert, brave

beetle highboards sawgrass into
swinging air — life is heavy, breath,
the trauma of butterflies.

INSIDE GEORGE STEINER

Of course it's hell: parsed sadness in an otherwise easy
weltanschauung. Like the summer we dreamt stalags not
sales tags, gathered old rooms like sheep, and by gather I
mean *bother*, a slight breeze shuffling waves, nothing more —
you think you're close, but just try touching them.

The minutiae are beautiful, but some consider them a sign
of fading out. You know: what grows wanes, what grows
in waning . . . Dutch courage of the privileged set (if they knew
what they were doing they'd know what's doing, and who).

No weak physics this, how we crowd our throats,
fill ourselves in emptying out, human spigots.
What else could we mean when we say this, this life
or boat, surf or passage, this *this*, this *is*, is difficult?
And isn't that just like us, to force such questions?

LAPSE

I can't see the widow in the garden —
black scarf glaring out the sun

I don't recall the swarm of fish —
garish mouths, little gasps of mud

I've forgotten the dice-box of thumbs —
their flight, fret and clatter down the hall

I've stopped thinking of the sea of thought —
weak peaks, flotsam in the swells

I can't remember that particular grey light
(you know the one)

that lingers on the pavement and
keeps the day from warming

LAWN JOCKEY

Someone has stolen the lawn,
replaced it with mere vegetation.
But how marvellous it is! — each
blade so differently the same,
its non-particularities fractured into
something reminiscent of a vast,
very well-maintained hairpiece —
the owner of which, of course, is

yours truly, musing after midnight,
not with that Chia Pet now propping
up the yard, but with my better organ,
one that's sworn off flogging resemblance,
just watching, really, my waking life run
naked over the gravestones of thought.

THE MOON IN THE BREAST OF MAN IS COLD

though half of us would say woman too, now,
if half of them half-heartedly, the balance pulling
binoculars from the nostalgia box, pointing
Poindexter lenses toward the southwest horizon and

imagining the one truly safe place north of Helsinki —
the shuttle glinting thumb's-width from the space station —
white-hot centre of everything 450 kilometres tall between
5:24 p.m. EST and the moment it falls into Earth's vast shadow.

The man who invented the hour must be replaced;
another starlet arrives dressed only in rose petals;
Winona needs a hand with all those handbags; the Baghdad
glee club ponders the absence of previously ticketed items.

And overhead, seven specks ride a knife of light
into the shoulder of everything, colder at every turn.

MORE EXTREME BLOOPERS OF THE MIDSUMMER FIREFLIES

Nothing a mob does is clean
　　　　— Les Murray

Whaddya know? Not much suffering out here
this p.m. — the gashes flanking the road have
healed up famously, scorch of gravel long
shimmered off — too weak to mount
much of a fight now anyway. No harm, no foul,
not even a grackle, the butterfly banquet
winding down, boozy petals waltzed on silk
wires, or like they should have been —
water thickening in the culverts, scarf of
wasps stumbling back to paper condos
before the blind throng emerges, like teen
lovers dodging curfew — unbottling
their petty firefight in the cornrows,

brief stars crashed over dry ears,
hushed and steepled in the sudden sight.

MOTIVE

You like it behind the dumpsters
Tuesdays, where it all spoils equally,
air pushes ripples through leaves
and repeats murmur after meaning.

Just as quickly you're thrilled with increment,
eighths, sevenths, half-hearted quarters:
a postponed collapse — pelting tines,
exhausted girders, vague words.

Vague words building a vague world,
framing spaces never quite addressed
where space itself is never quite itself,
though once perhaps it wanted to be.

Desiring the denigrations of change:
the rotating semaphore, pushed past
the weight of all of that other crap —
the zero-one-zero of breathing;

cluttered mirror, sad grammar
of full and empty; hard fact — breath
against abdication — the mad dash,
the dull, final, proud, inelegant null.

NO TREKKIE

The thing about pain is it's poetic.
Guess what I'm writing about.
You guessed it — how am I doing?
Sure, there are bigger issues, about which
we may all appear curious, great big
topics out there, I know it. But, truth is,
they're not so popular at the moment —
no one wants to hear it, all that office
politics and argy-bargy — no one takes
it out for lunch under the tall trees.
I invite my pain out for lunch under
the tall trees, show it how I've just put
"tall trees" under a line ending in
"under," you know, for *poetic* effect.
I tell my pain how much I admire it,
how empty my life would be if it left me.
"I need my pain," I say, and my pain
seems impressed, not realizing I am
quoting James Tiberius Kirk (clearly
my pain is no Trekkie, a relief, because it
means my pain will never show up
on Casual Day dressed as Doctor Crusher).
"*I need my pain,*" I whisper again, this time
very close, but it's obvious, my pain's not
listening. Its attention is held elsewhere;
it's dreaming of art, of love — grander
things. If only I'd known if only I'd
known if only I'd known . . .

A pink paper covers the "Reserved" ledger:
This Performance Oversold.
"You're sold out then?" I say to the Asian teller.
"Oh no," she whispers, "I give you a discount —
but don't tell anyone. They say it's not very good."
Dressed as candy stripers, pages arrive with pillows
for our shoes, tie laces, tape toes together, then toss
them wholesale down the elevator shaft.
When we're seated, it's onstage: me next to
the crib (in an unpainted chair I brought up
with me); Gil on a chaise too short for her legs.
I can wander to the door and watch the action,
but when she gets up, they panic, fuss her
hair up for her and escort her back to bed.

The play's called *The Gas Chamber*
by Samuel Beckett. In the main space, they're
bellowing into rubber cones dropped from
windblown clouds. There's miked belligerence
in the living room; backstage, actors bitch
about the restrictive costumes, slapping cheeks
harshly with their palms between scenes.
"[They arrive rosy-cheeked . . .]" one explains,
winking at me before plunging into another
domestic crucible. The audience is everywhere —
they are birds in the eaves, listeners by the elevator,
commotion in the foyer. Nearing the end, a flushed
patriarch approaches, angry, mopping his brow.

"All over then?" I suggest. "Time to go?"
"I think that would be best," he says.
"Best how?" I ask.
"Best, as in your best possible option,"
he replies, and not built for such upset,
turns tail and flees, weeping into his omnibus.

OPEN ALL NIGHT

Given all this misery, why the goofy smile?
Call it a run-on, stray, late bloomer. Or maybe
it's just a special night, under which a moon
leans in and nuzzles your shoulder, saying,

"Couldn't spare a bite of that burger could ya,
buddy? I mean, look at the *size* of you anyway."
Or maybe it stays put, its pallor suggesting
protein deficiency. Or it suddenly floats down,

kisses your neck, like some petal blown from Paris.
Maybe it's even true what they say: the real thing's
locked up in a CIA hangar in Arizona, this one
just a dirty searchlight sent to eat the hours.

Don't know, don't care, what with you glowering on the
other side of the glass: the old look, minus the usual pity.

OR WAS IT MY CREDENZA?

This great soporific sadness, if that's a word,
big, shabby, velveteen dog you won at the exhibition
but could have had twice over with the money
spent simulating a carnage of wildfowl.

And what good is it? For all its kiss, its little minnows
of window, vapour, vacationing snowflakes?
Take an option on the blizzard, bucket the buzzard,
take on the world in a circus run on nails.

You could fake it, but the weight loss pulls your
punches . . . pier at midnight . . . smooth noon as syntax.
Everyone's hands are beautiful to themselves:
scant hair flown into fields, windblown meadows.

Little vampires, tongues in the fount: it's my
credential they want, and they know they can have it.

PALEFACE

This? It's my *Dead by Dawn* look.
What do you think? All tarpaper and
bloody pigeons. A little fluid never hurt
anyone the Lord learned to help himself.
"Staunch" — an ugly word, even
for the dying, but then look at them,
crashed out in the waiting room watching
the method actors sweat. Get a ladder —
a tall one — with those non-slip rungs
you like so damned much.

Pull yourself in close when they toss me
down. See you at the bottom, pronto.

PHENOMENOLOGY

Force fingers into a
hot horizon — *bloodstains*

Drag leaves over the
leers of birches — *modesty*

Kick a glove through a
meadow of whispers — *disappointment*

Push the door past
panicking hinges — *possibility*

Thrust a cold arm into
a box of wind — *silence*

Drop lashes against a
squint of candle — *supernova!*

As scripted, a sun returns —
tenor for my garden of shards

POEM COMPOSED ON TEN LINES BY JOHN REED

Here it was absolutely dark, and nothing moved but pickets
of soldiers

In the lower hall, wailing and sounds of grief; the throng surged
back and forth before the bulletin board

People heaped on piles of lumber and bricks, perched high up on
shadowy girders, intent and thunder-voiced

Taking advantage of the diversion, we slipped past the guards
and set off in the direction of the Winter Palace

Delegations of starving cripples, orphans with blue, pinched
faces, besieged the building

I have listened in the breadlines, hearing the bitter, acrid note
of discontent

I heard one voice saying: "It is possible that we have done
wrong . . ."

Voices began to give commands and in the thick gloom we made
out a dark mass moving forward

Everybody was smiling; people ran into the streets holding out
their arms to the soft falling flakes, laughing

And in the rain, the bitter chill, the great throbbing city under
grey skies rushing faster and faster

Yes, I remember it clearly now:
I was taking the Serengeti photos into
the one-hour photo when some retarded
woman barrels into me with her laundry buggy.
I remember it distinctly: one of us said,
Where's the fire, brainless? And for the purposes
of this story, let's just say it was her.
Insulted, badly shaken, I report my injuries
to the security booth — not much sympathy
to go around there, what with the incessant bomb
scares and those missing brats from Flamenco Tots.
Won't even let me have one of their scooters
without a deposit and a handicapped sticker.

I'm about to go off on them when I recall
the words of the Mullah, whispered between
snaps of sailcloth on the mahogany skiff that
took us down the Nile on that unforgettable journey:
Never let a camel drink from your hip flask,
he said, or words to that effect — my weak Arabic
propped up by an out-of-date Fodor's and a copy
of *The Perfumed Garden* by Sir Richard Burton.
There are those who think on their feet,
but I've lost interest in being one of them, and
as I made my way calmly past Kernels
toward the whirling circus at Orange Julius
the welts under my shirt began to act up again.

Remembrances of the Bushmen's lash — I had
eaten a date they'd given me (first solid food
in weeks) and thrown away the pit,
thus violating their "use everything" policy
(backgammon counters, fishing floats,
napkin rings, fake eyes for the long dead).
Maybe it was just that my recent wounding
brought the whole ordeal back too keenly,

because a wince led to a sniffle, thence a sob,
then (in sequence) a moan, a cry, a rote and
futile entreaty to a cruel and discredited deity,
a mewl, and the inevitable disembodied shrieking
that shook the very bowels of the food court.

And as that brute escorted me through the main doors
to my vehicle, my hand strayed to the receipt in my
breast pocket and I was calmed by a certainty:
that inside 22 minutes my photos would be ready,
and this very evening they'd prompt profound reflection
on the many shades of that continental odyssey: the serene
faces of the beggar children, cruel shadows of the warlords,
flies hovering over that impossibly beautiful fruit.
All those tall, golden afternoons on the veldt.
I think it's the zebras I will miss the most —
their generosity, their homemade chardonnay,
their agility with a story, and the impressions . . .
Oh, the impressions!

REPOSSESSION

When they board up the hobby shop
only the moon notices — and the stationary
conductor waving in a train that no longer
circles the village, but is caught forever
in a chilly tunnel two peaks
north of the cheerless alpine church.

Down front, lead children
mock-shiver in the town square,
their little schnauzers parked mid-bark,
painted hands pawing for the rigid
mothers, painted sisters gathering wool
beside the Pop Shoppe.

Behind City Hall, past tumbleweed
flosses of silica snow, little train-model
glaziers slap train-model putty on train-
model trowels next to the lifelike factory,
where tradesmen stir simulated liquid
in a building without interior walls.

Out here in the genuine moonlight,
trees are still trees, light remains light,
and a die-cast freeway ducks the question,
closes up shop, turns its chair
toward the audience and bellows out
the sorry business of these worlds.

RISE AND SHINE

Whatever it is, *if* it is, it's always about
a mumble or a mutter or, very rarely,
a shout: on the stairs, among wet
branches, in the gaps between the things
amusing people say to drown us out;
all over these sheets even, in my own
undelivered whispers, which console only
me, and even then not for long.

Because truthfully, there's not much
to moan about, just the growing
preponderance of sheets, their almost
routine visits now established, their
inability to make sense of all this,
mutter cutting mutter as sky divides
branches or one follows zero, and is itself

followed by what you need to believe
might be anything — a wonder, even —
it's just that so far and seemingly by chance,
it's always, again, a one: a leaf, a table,
in a boardroom, at a window listening
for words that may not come, may never
have, and certainly not for you,
blue light waxing, stars guttered in
the brightness of that thought.

ROOMMATE

Hungry as a dress caught on low branches
you steer your cart of longing into the river.
Cold looks and sycophants — the choir practice
of middle age. No water in the hinges; still,
a creak, a crackle when you bend quickly,
dull bruise pealing weakly, an *abjectness*
— awkward word, yet there it is — like
the old roommate who knows too much,

witnessed the petty shames, might even
call you coward if he'd paid attention,
though by now you're pretty sure he never did.
And so you gamble, you dote, obfuscate;
drag a mat of needles onto the highway.
This form of pain is called composure.

RUMMAGE

Like a bee on a psychotropic leash,
a failed bid for buzz school,
Wednesday's bride is full of dread.
No one speaks of Kon-Tiki no more.
There are no eggs on Easter Island,
nil but creases on John Creasey's
theses, no legwork for Eric Ambler,
little left that's lean in Alistair MacLean.

Still, we'll bustle through the leaves, raffle
off the quilt. When it comes to recall, it's not
the height of the fall but the cut of the prat.
Like a metaphor most dire, like a dunk in a
half-stoked fire, I have tried in my ehs
to be Zed — and it makes me wander . . .

RUMSFELD SONATA

It's the squinty-kind physics teacher thing
that throws you, the hiss of thin skin
under the sensible suit. No question he's
enjoying it, this miscalculation of him,

as only someone who's been lowballed
all his life can — you learn a lot about living
living that close to the ground.
Bombs drop in my head, that other

market, where another Rumsfeld pushes
his paper aside, puts down his coffee
("Nothing special, hon', whatever's on sale")
and scribbles out a poem, his first ever:

He stretches out each conquering limb,
And then the small grass covers him.

SCIENTIFIC

Things fall apart, like the malaria on Kenny's
speed-dial, or the way the celestial widgets creak
to their predictable, irreversible close —
no dial tone, no car wreck, just the special treat
of watching the air beaten out of everything,

or at least the everything you love,
rising up, bumming quarters for mascots
and uniforms, fielding teams for which
you'll always be the last one picked.

There'll be no discount on shopworn jokes,
no peanuts furloughed from the heat lamp,
for all the singed fingers and the cancer scare.
The hedgerows scoff at our waffling:
clipboards, box elders, foot-faults, dentures . . .

SESTINA

Dirt and ugliness await me in the places I know.
The work of initiation cannot be hurried.
She began crying but she did not know why.
Mother's voice rising and falling, sometimes breaking off.
It was open when I touched it, and I held it to the twilight.
Shame lingered after the intimate scenes had vanished.

I *State*

Hatless, sorry-assed doubts — it was you all along:
the fragrant gutter of your wants winking fetchingly,
scaring up a wing chair, settling in for breakfast.
Which will *not* be forthcoming, not after the last time:
the bear-baiting and the spittoon — as if anyone would
fall for that tired gag: wind chimes for the old curmudgeons.

I'm in a state, though it isn't square or boot-shaped,
a jagged moon downsized yard by gaudy yard.
The debacle that is silence — we stand in line for it,
wish it well, pimp for it even, when the window
empties at 4 a.m. and there's nothing left to grieve
but the fissures in our faces, grown less and less singular.

The ball with the bell rolls drunkenly under the couch,
mother's voice rising and falling, sometimes trailing off.

II *Indulgences*

We stood there panting, gathering ourselves for action,
while the plummets optioned and Gus the Birthday Clown
alienated everyone with his chain-smoking and those dog-shaped
balloons. Dust gathered under the Instacopy, the no-account
counter help picked pimento from the chicken loaf while
we stood there, panting, gathering ourselves for action.

Years pass and we're poised to clone Christ.
Just to be certain, we take scrapings from a dozen of the
oldest souvenirs. Within months, three of four samples reveal
a tiny replica of one Alfred Wolfram of Dauphin, Manitoba.
"It's our mistakes that define us," he'll say later in scores
of televised addresses. "We adore them, to be totally honest."

And so we dawdle, knocking tines from a chandelier of sorrows.
Dirt and ugliness await us in the places we know.

III *Bridge*

The long yellow hallway with the doors sewn shut
bellows its chest, flames the dormitory with fury.
Conspiracies are child's play once you pigeonhole
the weak links — be it bar stool or stool pigeon,
creeping doubt throws up its dull mug suddenly,
just before someone with high-end duds gets well

and truly fucked. Like a meek toenail who returns to
the playground at midnight, looking for the prick who
called him "moonface," I'll stare down my worries.
Parcels of dreaming traffic, on a bridge, after years of
misery, a sudden glimpse of happiness, like the dry
pant of tape recorders, waved over the dead.

It was spring, and all the sprinklers were turned on.
Shame lingered after the intimate scenes had vanished.

IV *Crepuscular*

Dread hectors a guileless morning into full confession.
It was no biggie anyway, a few fake clouds, several
kited cheques, nothing the god of cybergenetics would
keep you out of heaven for. Of course, there's also
the sinister disappearance of everything kind and gentle:
a long yellow hallway with the doors sewn shut.

Walk it off, but the pace stays the same — brisk —
kick and jump, kick and jump, extra stride before
the water hazard, then over: watch the time, no faults yet,
LINE
LINE
the chess masters evacuated under cover of darkness.

Frantic scrabbling, a kafuffle in the shadow cabinet.
It was open when I touched it, and I held it to the twilight.

V *Middle Management*

I'm in a state, though it isn't square or boot-shaped
so that rules out Florida, Italy, and most variety meats.
You hatless sorry-assed doubts, it was you all along
propping up middle management, making lions of the
maggots, while the spam piles up, and productivity plummets
into an engineered swoon, that is, an engineered swoon.
The marigolds of autumn swan home, draw themselves
a bath; despair strides the garage like genuine climate.

As though there ever was a cue, or a truly elegant exit:
under the radar, over the falls and back to shore unharmed,
the leaf insect who caught the magic raindrop.
Truth told, there are always consequences, though like
attractive babysitters, we all seem to take each other's home.
She began crying, but she couldn't have known why.

VI *Tall Ships*

Like the dry pant of tape recorders waved over the dead,
it's a dirty trick. To be given all this, then snatch it away.
In the south they paint time into corners, rush it, bellow
at it, stick their cocks in and dare it to be done.
Up here we stare it down — think things to a stalemate.
We'll all get our curtain call, though few have what
you'd really call an act: Guy at the Coke Dispenser,
Babe Serving Thin-Crust Pizza, Dude Selling Charity

Coupon Booklets; Girl Removing Dead Mexican Jumping Beans
and Replacing Them with Live Mexican Jumping Beans.
Dread hectors the guileless morning into full confession,
though none of it's admissible. In the end, we're all bores:
space-filler, errant name tags, plates cleared from the buffet.
Golfers strewn like sailboats over the pitiless greens.
The work of initiation cannot be hurried.

S.E.T.I.

Up there, out in real space, past the sour milk
of metaphor, beyond the innuendoes of ice, I
imagine a race so visionary that each
evolves into a single eye, the perfect peepers run on
filaments that are (to the cones of our retina) as
that famous palace in India is to a garden shed.
As their sight developed (tired of stumbling),
they lost use of their legs, shed their arms (so none
could know the pain of a lover holding another)
and, after considerable public debate, abandoned
even the televisions they had once loved
(that same myopic actor staring back).

For entertainment, they'd look to the real history
sparkling overhead, collective irises a windsock
blown over the stars from some glorious desert,
until each minute speck on this ancient dot
was refined and refocused in real time. Nothing
unusual going on here, really, a half-serious air-guitar
session, evening of ironing, debate over who goes
where for what — but a sudden sense of alien fame,
a random attention to you, particularly, wound up
and frustrated, walking a block then glaring at
the buses passing, your expression untranslated
and oddly ugly, nothing useful on your mind,
having perished all those eons ago.

SETTLEMENTS

Fragments of a footstep, door-knock, a berth
of empty sleepers. Where conscience reigns,
mules dream deeper — thoughts tossed
willy-nilly under the panoply of drowsy sighs.
Scour the antidote for breathing: not the
fissures, but the squirrelled patents, the
duds that peacock after morning.
Cue the flash floods, flush the chisellers out,
cut the power on their feral children.
Big schemes draw big shakers —
shepherd logic, sticks and scowls.
We resist, but in the pinch, go quietly.

They've built forests for such settlements.
We could meet there.

SLEEPING AT THE OFFICE

Those who weren't afraid are now afraid,
though we express our fears differently,
some by being scared, some by printing T-shirts.
In the food court 120 stories deep
the dead lie roped and smoking —
the doggers hiding in the lunchroom,
keeners who stayed at their desks,
the too slow, unlucky, too helpful;
the ones who heard the all-clear, turned

in the stairwell and scuffled up against the
flow. Some of them are still climbing:
New York's finest — 300 plus —
when the sky dropped they improvised:
divvied up hoses and shimmied back to bed.
Those on wings, tearing in like confetti,
theirs was cleanest, a *Sweet Jesus*,
a *Yes, I see*, breath coughed in an ear
before the rift in the air opened fire
and erupted, no sensible way back.

They say it's easy in your sleep; slip out
on a pretext — early meeting, fictional client,
improbable tryst. The days dumbed down to
nomenclature, sequence, orbits taped to skin.
Anything that can be learned is learned fast:
apprehension, acquiescence, blurred plummet
— all the pretty brokers dozing at their terminals,
dreaming of a time there was time.

SO FAMILIAR

after Darrell Gray

You are the toy delivered at daybreak,
conundrum to a storm of check marks,

and still, so familiar to me
this bale of regret
I have strawdogged . . .

Cordwood, filibuster,
young love caught under the porch
with the chamois and the millionaire

A class of oafs
can set the terms more finely
than any time-share Nero

But when I put up my fiddle, the
moon dawdles on my cheekbones —
all those plump hours tractoring back

SPACE SONNET

though a post impounds the rising moon
there's no harm in the fence, just doing its job:
carving everything tethered to earth into loose
squares, then setting all that's free in motion

that moon, for instance, unharmed, not-quite-
inflated beachball with the celebrated pizza-
face, rising off a pinpoint like the last bubble
tumbled from the lip of some ancient sailor

he read the tides from the gleeless face,
wrote his love under its damp blue lamp,
huge and almost catchable as it busted out,
wan and fading, ever colder in its rising,

like it knows — the gauze of closeness
pales given the charisma of distance

SPELL G.O.D.

> *The world will soon break up into*
> *small colonies of the saved*
> — Robert Bly

The bluebirds in their beige hours nodding;
nothing reasoned nothing reined, the dire
quarrel put by until brunch, another polite
tiff over forcemeats and poaching limits.

Wherefore art thou, rodeo? Not your average
dong presiding over the hazmats and the
gone gone gone. Whittle it down, Georgie.
Yank the big chain back and stare it in the

mangle — this fabulous accident, planes
descending firebrand over the hard knocks
and the breezy frieze. Where's the club pro?
Whither wherewithal? What gives, really?

The shred cry of metal crescending —
grind it up, dogs, you pounds of freedom.

STILL LIFE WITH PIGEON

and in the distance, the distance . . .
                    — James Tate

Because the morning is dull I dislike this
pen, but can't find the one that wrote
the better summer. The sky opens slowly,
like a handicapped door, like nothing but

done wrong — yet here it comes, the advertised
vista, a little addled by the recent geopolitical
upheaval, yet still willing to lick a little ass,
even advance, modestly, in this company

so long as it doesn't suck up every weekend.
Birthday clown (al fresco), twitchy pigeons, those
melting things (what are they called?) — such are
the approved shenanigans, even if they seem a tad,

well . . . studied . . . like polio, or that cheap
plastic owl that's supposed to make us tremble.

SWALLOWING

Unspoiled, most schedules fly here:
the flies leave the fields, the fields
lie fallow, we watch swallows fly low,
one swallow swallows a fly —
a circle always seems glamorous
until it's you doing the swallowing.
Pre-sunup, dark mesas reign,
then the windmills appear —
semaphore — remote viewing
from back of beyond.

We're all perverts when it comes
down to it, we'll all open our coats
to the right stranger, codes hidden
in our pants, our junk, our junkets.
A good lunch calms the wary,
a shuttle launch cheers the aging,
a blue joke charms the jailors,
your neighbours . . . pleased to meet you.

There's weather over the smoke pit —
things go all thundery, then stop.
Blue balls, blue bonnets, yellow jackets —
it's all so Wide Open here —
night is a big girl's blouse, hovering
over the smiling beach of a dentist.

SWALLOWS

It would almost be worth it, he thinks — basting a chicken
on a gas grill with a beer can up its ass, swallows diving
in the evening light — to have four years instead of forty, eight
instead of eighty (no longevity stats on swallows forthcoming),

to *move* like that, hit a rogue current, throw up your flag and
hang with it, hollow-boned acrobat that you are. To be
tossed over the gloom and lightning, properly terrified
of your speed, your height, for as tall and thirsting as your fame

no ground can claim you, no stone so fast and hard and fleeting
though the air flirts hard and the tan light gives it legs.
Swallow enough anything and it's euphoria. Strangled or
drowned, we all die drunk — no vexed loves, no stowed

slights, just a hole at the top of a column that thunders and
beckons and brightens, then, tightening, flees the scene.

TEN CENTS A DANCE

I was unlike a pack of dollar-store batteries;
unlike the subway stuttering, incoherent.
I was unlike a woman chasing a fleeing schnauzer,
unlike a shadow on the butcher's window.

I was unlike a bird, not that bird . . . the pretty one . . .
unlike an old joke grown warm in the telling.
I was unlike the milkman, stopped visiting years ago.
I was unlike anything I remotely dreamt of being —

unlike a lake filled with menaced boats,
unlike bowling, Yahtzee, a bag of stale pastries.
I was unlike the beard on this polite, turbaned salesman;
I was unlike my old likenesses in so many ways.

It was oddly liberating — I mean, it felt good — but,
in another way, the saddest thing I ever imagined.

TENNIS, ELBA

Catgut, smoked meats, headlands, headgear —
such things have been so dumbed down, derailed —
take the game of tennis, for example, which used to
be a complex yet genteel pastime involving a net, a lake
and a flightless cabbage you called Norman or Edam
depending on which side of the racket you were standing.
Match ended, the vanquished was bought a boxed lunch,
whereas the winner got doused in fire and tasked
with a prickling, malodorous sweater.
No, the champions of the Golden Age would not
recognize their noble game in what is played today,
with its roadies and ice follies, its obscure
funding formulae and tired film-noir analogies.
If not for the occasional glimpse of toned ham and
glittery undergarments: colossal waste of time.
What we might need, and I agree such ideas are
never popular, but let me just reiterate that what
we *might* need is a strong leader, like Napoleon
or Veronica Lake, someone whose name probably
isn't even their real name, but who knows how to toss
back her blonde mane and invade Russia on a
whim, kiss Alan Ladd on his thin lips and retire to
Elba, secret pain tucked into a coat flap
with the bruised wing and the skin condition.

To think like Diana or golf — live by the screw and die
by the driver. To stop litany cold, like *that*, mid-sentence.
To paraphrase a certain sea bream I used to drink with,
that's where the schooling comes in. Start with a ton of planks
and replace them with other currents; hammerhead a platform
and keep it fed on plankton, strained through a series of
escalating sieves. Canvass the brush-offs and weak excuses,
stir a reluctant electorate with tales of nautical victory.
Lake, though adorable, flatly refused to align her many
swells and crash against that thoughtless net of sand.
Bonaparte was never blown apart, though he *was* slowly

poisoned by that same hand he played so close to the vest —
and invented the French judicial system as we know it today,
including its penchant for bad boys, its sultry, measured purr,
glamorous tumble down a set of stares, and the windswept
cliff of a modest narrow-brimmed hat once popular with
banisters, sharp cheeses, delinquent swains and those
wizened yellow despots we used to call sultanas.

THIS JUST IN

You can't leave anything out —
the cat will get it, like the spring
light gets the rose bush in the end,

whether its thorned arms grab for shade
or not. No cover for anything now the
snow's hopscotched back to the sewers
clogged with water, running home.

Push hard enough and just about anything
will push right back — sun and shade, yard
birds, wire fence, compost bucket, dirty ball,
that sweet scent under the leaves and shit.

It's not light, but memory, that crashes off
the screen window and rolls under the door
— you can't leave anything out.

THUNDERING ABSENCE

after James Tate

The problem of breath in our age:
there is no current pure enough;
no, there is no vacuum a gust
won't fawn over, unflappable
as they are, the thundering absences
in airports, in love with a stationary
armchair.
    Oh vermin of commerce! There is
no total at the end of the invoice.
There is no invoice. Blight
accrues like boiling digits,
with not a wink for anyone.

VIRGINIA BEACH

With all that used netting around, why go plastic?
Another biggie question left unanswered when you're
fleeing winter; though it's true, the hotter things get,
the more the military wants a piece of it, kinking up
the beer funnels, busting up the keggers with

a triple shot of "What you thinking, chief?"
Duh . . . we *thought* we were getting laid, that is before
the tequila slowed things down to a fruity slur.
F-16s chase invisible midges over the cotton swells,
a righteous honey spoons crab salad from a giant bugle.

A school of skipjacks hits the effluent current, turns tail
and runs, haunted by the wayward shoal of light.
The effect of things young on the suddenly aging —
Krakatoa bursting in the tiny minds of giants.

WOMAN . . . CAREENING

Love. If you're smart you'll dowse yourself in it.
It's the marble cakewalk, the best thing going.
It's $100 wings-and-champs for everyone, at
least the everyone parked late on detail shift,
crossing aitches, dotting esses and still not moo-
shooing the secretary, despite the warm reception.

Plate it up, dudes; roll the dice clear into the
little boy's room if you're moved to. If this be the
glove department, whither the stuttering prince?
Does he curtsy on the ramparts? Do you stock
his mauve in ermine? Does he pause, perplexed,
yet frantic for those words he ordered?

Brunette with cut flowers careening into traffic,
settling it: what starts the heart stops the world.

WRITE WHAT YOU KNOW

Some of the poems in this book may first seem to the reader like dramatic monologues or poems written in a persona, and, in fact, that was exactly the intention.

"Contractual Obligation" was written after a stint as "host" at some events of the Harbourfront International Festival of Authors in October 2002. Thanks again to Greg Gatenby for the gig (and the poem).

"Drift" was inspired, in part, by a painting of the same name by Toronto artist Nestor Kruger. The epigraph is from Wisława Szymborska's "Reality Demands," from *View with a Grain of Sand: Selected Poems* (Harcourt Brace, 1995), translated by Stanisław Barańczak and Clare Cavanagh.

"Eels" is after Gösta Ågren's "Childhood Summer," in *A Valley in the Midst of Violence: Selected Poems* (Bloodaxe, 1992), translated by David McDuff.

"Errata" is after a poem of the same name by Paul Muldoon in *Hay* (Farrar, Straus and Giroux, 1998).

The epigraph for "Half of Something" is from David Berman's poem "Now II," from *Actual Air* (Open City, 1999).

The last image in "History Channel" was drawn from a detail in Don DeLillo's novel *Libra* (1988).

"Hooks" is a gloss on Darrell Gray's "Prongs," from *Something Swims Out* (Blue Wind, 1972).

The title of "The Moon in the Breast of Man Is Cold" is from the last line of John Berryman's poem "The Moon and the Night and the Men" (1940), which can be found in *Collected Poems 1937–1971* (Farrar, Straus and Giroux, 1989).

The epigraph for "More Extreme Bloopers of the Midsummer Fireflies" is from Les Murray's poem "Demo," in *Subhuman Redneck Poems* (Noonday/Farrar, Straus and Giroux, 1997).

"Motive" is a gloss on Wallace Stevens's "The Motive for Metaphor," which can be found in just about any anthology of modern American poetry. The author is mindful of the implied hubris.

The first line of "Paleface" was inspired by the opening of Bill Kushner's poem "Up," from *Head* (United Artists, 1986).

"Poem Composed on Ten Lines by John Reed" is a collage of passages from Reed's *Ten Days That Shook the World* (1919). The order, length, and punctuation are mine, otherwise the lines are reproduced verbatim.

The last line of "Roommate" was inspired by the last line of Gösta Ågren's poem "Summer," from *A Valley in the Midst of Violence: Selected Poems* (Bloodaxe, 1992), translated by David McDuff.

The last two lines of "Rumsfeld Sonata" are from Louis Untermeyer's "Long Feud," from *Modern American Poetry and Modern British Poetry, Combined Mid-Century Edition* (Harcourt, Brace and Company, 1950), edited by Louis Untermeyer.

"Settlements" is for Walid Bitar.

"So Familiar" is a gloss on Darrell Gray's poem "So Strange to Me," from *Halos of Debris* (Poltroon Press, 1984).

The epigraph for "Spell G.O.D." is from Robert Bly's poem "Those Being Eaten by America," from *The Contemporary American Poets* (Mentor/New American Library, 1969), edited by Mark Strand.

"Thundering Absence" is a homolinguistic translation of James Tate's "Suffering Bastards," in *Hints to Pilgrims* (University of Massachusetts Press, 1971).

ACKNOWLEDGEMENTS

Grateful acknowledgement is made to the editors of the publications in which the following poems first appeared, often in slightly different form:

"The Gradualists," "So Familiar," "Spell G.O.D.," and "Swallowing," in *Chicago Review*
"Harmless Rituals," in *dig*
"No Trekkie" and "Contractual Obligation," in *This Magazine*
"Lapse," in *Taddle Creek*

"Repossession," "Drift," "Contractual Obligation," "Hooks," "Deposition," "Architect," "In Limbo," "Finger Lake," and "Indulgences" appeared in the anthology *Surreal Estate* (Mercury Press, 2004). Thanks to Stuart Ross and Bev Daurio for including me in that project.

This book was greatly assisted (and accelerated) by a grant from the Canada Council for the Arts and several smaller grants from the Ontario Arts Council through its Writers' Reserve Program. Thanks to both institutions and to citizens of both jurisdictions who support the sometimes less-than-unanimous proposition that art is something important enough to be given public money.

On a personal note, I'd like to especially thank Gil Adamson for her love, great faith, great brain, great ear, and constant encouragement; my editor, Ken Babstock (who's done me more good turns than I can ever repay), for his big heart and bigger talent; Bill Douglas and Eamon Mac Mahon for the gorgeous cover; Michael Holmes for his enthusiasm and generosity in reading an earlier version of this book; Lynn Crosbie and Jen LoveGrove for their support and friendship; Ron Silliman for the heads-up on Darrell Gray and others; Nate Dorward for the copy-edit; and my dear friend Stuart Ross, who works cheap, and who put me in touch with the work of many of the poets who were the inspiration for so much of this book.

Thanks also to Martha Sharpe, Laura Repas, Kevin Linder, Matt Williams, Sarah MacLachlan, and everyone else at Anansi for being so good at what they do, and for making me feel at home.